Little BIG Girl

By Amanda Cobb-Greetham

Illustrated by Danielle R. Fixico

ISBN 978-1-952397-22-6 (hardcover)
ISBN 978-1-952397-21-9 (paperback)

Book design by Jackson Davis
Printed in Canada

Chickasaw Press
PO Box 1548
Ada, Oklahoma 74821
chickasawpress.com

To AJ, Stella, Connor, Hobo, Jack, and Lila Lee.
—Amanda Cobb-Greetham

A Note from the Author

My husband, Stephen, and I have adopted six rescue dogs over the course of our years together. We have loved them all dearly, but we haven't always known much about their lives before they came to us.

Cuddly AJ and Jack, a Golden Retriever and Australian Shepherd respectively, were surrendered by their original owners into pet foster care organizations after they were found to have health issues—epilepsy and blindness. Stephen found Stella, a proud and independent Lab/Husky in a shelter, just a few days away from being euthanized. Connor, the loyal Lab, spent the first year of his life chained to a tree before finding his foster family, while Lila Lee and over a dozen other Pyrenees puppies were found abandoned in the country and searching for food. Hobo—a dog like no other—just showed up in our yard one rainy day and stayed. We are glad we found them, and we are forever grateful they found us!

In this book, Little Girl—who shares many personality traits with Lila Lee—has lost her family. Although the story has a happy ending, Little Girl is not reunited with her original family. This surprised a few people—wouldn't children want her to find her family? The answer is yes, children do want her to find her family—a forever family.

Sometimes children—just like Little Girl—go through very hard times in life. It is my hope that this story will give you and the children in your life the opportunity to talk about experiences like loss of a loved one, adoption, or foster care, as well as feelings we all share, like fear and safety, loss and hope, loneliness and belonging, and love. *Little Big Girl* just might make your family laugh, cry, and . . . adopt a dog!

Little Girl curled up in the corner against the concrete wall, listening to the rain. She squeezed her eyes tight shut and tried to remember HOME.
It was getting harder and harder to remember.

She remembered OUTSIDE—

chasing bright butterflies,
digging up wiggly worms,
snapping off tasty little twigs,
and bark-Bark-**BARKING** at her froggy friend.

Then, she remembered INSIDE—nibbling on snacky,
bite-sized, bits, snoozing on the fuzzy blanket,
bark-Bark-BARKING at the doorbell,
and best of all,
cuddling during nap time!

She also remembered LOST.
LOST was TOO cold,
TOO lonely,
and TOO scary to think about.

SHELTER was better than LOST.
But it still wasn't HOME.

Maybe—just maybe—she would meet a family at the
Pet Adoption Fair tomorrow—a nice family
who would take her HOME.

Week after week, she and the other puppies would go to the park to meet families, and week after week, families would adopt the puppies—but not Little Girl. She was TOO BIG.

Little Girl didn't understand. She was TINY—the very smallest puppy in her litter. Everyone said so. Sometimes, they had even called her runt! No, there was no way she could be TOO BIG.

It was all very confusing, but tomorrow,
she would show a nice family just how little she was.
Then, they would take her HOME.
Just thinking about it made Little Girl warmer and happier.

She decided it was time to stop remembering and start
sleeping so tomorrow would come fast.

Little Girl spun with excitement.
Families were coming down the sidewalk!

Adopt a puppy!

A nice family would see her
and take her **HOME**, she just knew it.
Here I am! Here I am!

"Don't you think she's TOO BIG?"
"Definitely."
"We want to take home a little puppy."

And they walked right past her.

Little Girl couldn't believe her ears! She was not **TOO BIG**. How could she show them? Little Girl bark-Bark-**BARKED** just as loud as she could, pull-Pull-**PULLED** until her leash snapped, and scrambled through the mud to the family.

She hopped up on her hind legs and hugged them hard.
See? She was so much smaller than they were.
"That puppy is **TOO BIG**," they said.
And they pushed Little Girl away.

Little Girl sat behind a big, leafy tree and watched them unwrap lunch. She was not **TOO BIG**. How could she show them? Little Girl hurried to the table and helped herself to a bite of their sandwich.

See?
She was so little she hardly ate anything!
"She is **TOO BIG!**" they said.
And they shooed her away.

Little Girl rolled on her back in the wet grass under the tree and thought about what to do next.
More than anything, she wanted HOME.
She was not TOO BIG.
How could she show them?

How can I show them?

With a running start, Little Girl leapt on the bench, landing right in their laps. See?
She was so small she hardly took up any room at all. She snuggled up, just like she used to, and...

"OFF!" they said.
UP jumped the family, and **DOWN** came Little Girl,
right on the ground!
"You are **TOO BIG!**" they said.
And they walked away.

Little Girl curled up on the sidewalk and squeezed her eyes tight shut. She couldn't bear to watch them fold up the tables and take down the signs. She reminded herself that **SHELTER** was better than **LOST**.

But not much better. She didn't understand.
She knew in her heart that she wasn't TOO BIG
and then she heard...
"I hope we find a puppy who likes to run and play OUTSIDE."
"I hope we find a puppy who likes to snuggle INSIDE."
I hope we are not too late," the family said. "We'd better hurry!"
Little Girl could not believe her ears! The fair was over.
The families were gone. She must be dreaming.

"It's her!" they shouted, "It's her!"
The voices sounded so real, she decided to risk a little peek.
Little Girl opened her eyes and looked into the
smiling eyes of a nice family.

"She's so muddy!" they laughed.
"She definitely likes to play OUTSIDE! I'll bet she likes to snuggle up INSIDE, too," they said, rubbing Little Girl's tummy.
"She's such a LITTLE puppy for such a BIG breed of dog."

"She's JUST RIGHT," the family said.
"She's our LITTLE BIG GIRL."

Little Big Girl bounded across the grass,
chasing bright butterflies,
digging up wiggly worms,

snapping off tasty little twigs,
and bark-Bark-**BARKING** at her best bunny friend.
How she loved **OUTSIDE**.

She loved INSIDE too!
Nibbling on snacky, bite-sized, bacon bits,
snoozing on the fuzzy blanket,

bark-Bark-**BARKING** at the doorbell...

But the very best place of all,
whether INSIDE or OUTSIDE,
was right HERE...

Little Big Girl was HOME!

Let's BARK About It!

Little Big Girl provides families an opportunity to identify and discuss complex emotions with children. Use the questions below to springboard meaningful conversations about feelings with your family!

1. At the shelter, Little Girl remembers what it felt like to be lost and sad, but also feels hopeful about the pet adoption fair. What makes you feel better when you're sad?

2. Little Girl wanted a family to take her home. What does home mean to her? What does home mean to you?

3. Many families from the pet adoption fair thought that Little Girl was too big—bigger than the other puppies. Has there been a time where you didn't fit in? How did that feel?

4. Little Girl is excited to ride home in the car with her forever family. What do you get excited about?

5. Little Girl loves to play outside and be cozy inside. What are some things you love?

6. Does your family have a dog, cat, or other pet? How did you meet your pet? Are they similar or different to Little Girl?

Amanda Cobb-Greetham

Amanda Cobb-Greetham, a Chickasaw citizen from Oklahoma, is a long-time university professor and the award-winning author of *Listening to Our Grandmothers Stories: The Bloomfield Academy for Chickasaw Females*. She was instrumental in launching the Chickasaw Cultural Center (2007-2012) and the Chickasaw Press (2007), has been honored as Chickasaw Nation Dynamic Woman of the Year (2018), and was inducted into the Chickasaw Hall of Fame (2023). She was excited to collaborate with her former student, Danielle R. Fixico, on *Little Big Girl*.

She and her husband, Stephen, spend their time in Oklahoma and North Carolina, where she serves as Distinguished Professor at the University of North Carolina-Chapel Hill. They love their dogs very much.

Photo by Stephen Greetham

Lila Lee

Lila Lee, also known as Baby Girl and Little Big Girl, is a ninety-seven-pound bundle of fluff and happiness who found her forever family almost four years ago. She enjoys barking, snacking, napping, snuggling, getting belly rubs, and playing with her brother, Jack. She loves everyone and everything, and especially loves her HOME.

 To learn more about pet adoption, go to aspca.org or humanesociety.org.

Photo by Stephen Greetham

Danielle R. Fixico

Danielle Fixico is a Chickasaw, Muscogee, and Choctaw artist from Morris, Oklahoma, whose work focuses on raising awareness for women's issues in First American communities. She received both a master of fine arts in painting and a bachelor's degree in Native American studies from the University of Oklahoma, and serves as an adjunct fine art professor at the College of the Muscogee Nation.

Danielle was a 2022-2023 Center for Native American Youth Remembering Our Sisters fellow and has been featured in a variety of publications and events, including the National Day of Awareness for Missing and Murdered Indigenous Women (MMIW). She has been exhibited in an array of galleries, which include the Fred Jones Jr. Museum of Art and Exhibit C Gallery. If she isn't painting away in her studio or spending time with family, you can find her in the backyard playing fetch with her two pups, Malatha and Hiloa.

Photo by Wiley Barnes